BUTTS, BLEPS, AND BEANS CAT COLORING BOOK

BUTTS, BLEPS, AND BEANS

CAT

COLORING BOOK

35 COLORING PAGES FOR ADULTS

ILLUSTRATED BY LIZZIE PRESTON

ROCKRIDGE
PRESS

For general information on our other products and services or to obtain technical support, please contact our Customer Care Department within the United States at (866) 744-2665, or outside the United States at (510) 253-0500.

Rockridge Press publishes its books in a variety of electronic and print formats. Some content that appears in print may not be available in electronic books, and vice versa.

TRADEMARKS: Rockridge Press and the Rockridge Press logo are trademarks or registered trademarks of Callisto Media Inc. and/or its affiliates, in the United States and other countries, and may not be used without written permission. All other trademarks are the property of their respective owners. Rockridge Press is not associated with any product or vendor mentioned in this book.

Interior and Cover Designer: Lindsey Dekker
Art Producer: Hannah Dickerson
Editor: Brian Sweeting
Production Editor: Emily Sheehan
Illustrations © 2020 Collaborate Agency/Lizzie Preston

ISBN: Print 978-1-64611-842-7
R0

This coloring book belongs to:

_____

Introduction

Cats may seem sophisticated and alluring, but sometimes they can't help sticking out a tiny tongue or baring a furry behind. Familiarize yourself with these feline phrases and have fun coloring in all the peculiar kitty characteristics that make cats unique:

 BUTTS. In certain social circles, a rump might cause a ruckus, but cats show off their butts when they're feeling friendly. Don't be offended by an exposed posterior—it's a sign of trust and affection.

 BLEPS. Sticking out an itty-bitty bit of tongue is more than just a cutesy photo pose, it's also how cats detect scents around them.

 BEANS. The adorable little paw pads on the underside of a cat foot.

 BOOPS. The sweet, affectionate touch of a cat nose is a sign of great trust.

 SPLOOTS. The ultimate sign of relaxation, this stretch happens when a kitty lays down with legs extended back like a frog.

 FLOOFS. A cat that is looking particularly light, fluffy, and furry is for *sure* a floof.

 TEEFIES. Small and sharp and cute and out, sometimes a cat likes to show off its chomps.

 LOAVES. No, not freshly baked bread, a loaf is a fluffed up furball with paws and tail tucked comfortably beneath.

 SMOL. When a cat is tiny and little and small, it is also *smol*.

 IF I FITS, I SITS. No space is too tight for a kitty to squeeze into—boxes, sinks, shoes, bowls, and vases all make cozy seats.

BUTT

BUTT

BUTT

BUTT

BUTT

BUTT

BUTT

BLEP

BLEP

BLEP

BLEP

BEANS

BEANS

BEANS

BEANS

BEANS

BOOP

BOOP

BOOP

SPLOOT

SPLOOT

SPLOOT

FLOOF

FLOOF

TEEFIES

TEEFIES

LOAF

LOAF

LOAF

SMOL

SMOL

IF I FITS, I SITS

IF I FITS, I SITS

IF I FITS, I SITS

IF I FITS, I SITS

About the Illustrator

LIZZIE PRESTON is a designer, illustrator, and creative from Birmingham, United Kingdom. She has a love for all things design and has a BA in graphic design from Nottingham Trent University. She has experience working with a greeting card company in Northamptonshire and enjoys freelancing as a designer. Her style is versatile and includes everything from doodles to laser cuts, graphics, and hand drawings. She also has a passion for typography and intricate illustrations.

CPSIA information can be obtained
at www.ICGtesting.com
Printed in the USA
JSHW012018191121
20578JS00004BA/6